11th Hour

Jonathan Hallam
Anastasia Freygang

the old fish in the thai restaurant in the north died finally after years of the family giving it salad, which sank slowly through the water only to be snatched with precision by a big haul.

this found an end.

he ate like a man, carried his weight in the tank like a mammal. and died being remembered.

in my head i am filming you. in my head you speak riddles to the thai family and eventually speak out a last good goodbye and sink to the ground.

your worldly body is the only one in this aquarium while we cruise the streets in restlessness, floating about to the next hurt and the next crowd. to the next idea for survival and for pleasure. for mojo times of no reproduction to reach eventually reproduction and then we see the life's cycle and cry. cry for you and for us, for the sky over the city and the water raging by the banks. once again we collapse in our lovers arms and think of the future.

in such moments the past rattles like a soundtrack in our mind reminding us of our lives and of the ones that we have lost and the ones we will never see again.

while birds lay eggs we plunge into doctors hands but i saw her
going up a mountain
her smile resonated while her spiritual brother cheered

whose child you carry doesn't matter

between
ceilings in vertical perception
the closing happens
wherever you go you must have trust
the penetration happens
it's dreaming of breaking
gathering the recreational tools is part one
on the path to resurrection

flying burning phoenix word with this very meaning hitting the sky that means the world

call it mental breakthrough
levelling voice. be aware that words are prayers.

yourself cried a river for sadness' sake
being abandoned
interchanges with abundance
seeing the given
hallelujah

words of young souls' wisdom
body of young soul seeking saving grace

you wonder who ought to hear this
who ought to give a hand

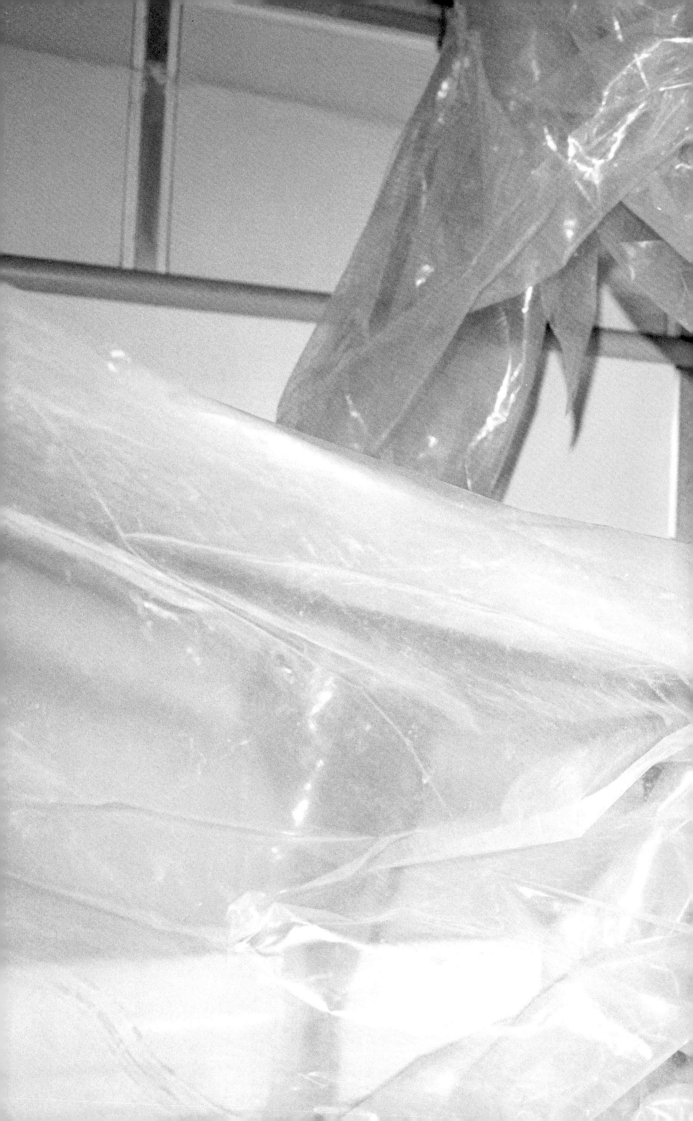

reconstructing the skeleton of your learning.
your trauma. your life and death can be your path to consciousness.

the next knowing occurs
the next seeing in context
the other for realm's expansion marks the buddy
relating back in astonishment
times
to figures
to senses

all of this
prone to be providing linkings

lucky love straight into you from teenage heaven

chancers strive and enchant. lets try this.
fuck everything that doesn't make you happy

the heart that learned so many things

to relate back one must unfold the happenings untold, just learned and experienced.
know your craving curiosity has a karmic stance. progress, process and rewind

marking a point in time you manifest physically
mentally to follow, habit creates ethos
dealing it, head on. re- awakening

burning candles out
for darkness pumping the space as an entity
for you to submerge into your own entity
blind you are tracing your breath into your stomach and reach out for embrace

who ever is near
and warm and calm

conditions of the mind
translate to the outer
tuning in believing

waveye
you focus
riddles unfold
you have trust

you regather lust particles for blooming
rise and strive, revealing

meeting on meeting
rencontre on a cloud with sunbeams piercing your tears
falling like a fountain upwards
you are pushing the pain out

we move to places taking out the essence of our surroundings by
constructing sense anew and being awake in the now
we are forcing nowness through wondrous eyes
when each smile meets a receptor we fold up our past and throw
it regardless of its attachment to the heart and we try to start anew

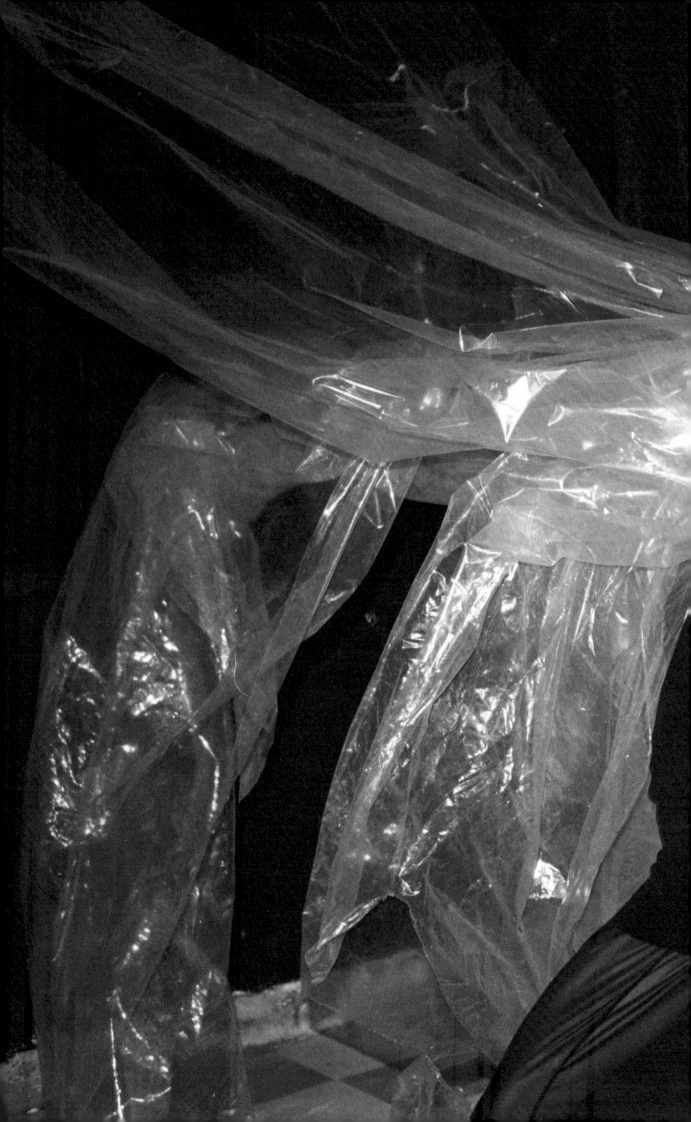

grief and resurrection

.

the female power. the goddess
über mother
cranky boys feeding off it

i reject your inner child. your dependency. i cry out to stay alive, protesting.
why hanging on to her. how things turn in years.
the protector meets her vulnerable followers.
not wanting followers but wanting to embrace the lovers.

the eyes that speak time. wise and observing.
knowing people and their flaws. wanting nothing.

thin skin around the hands, bones, knuckles. faded tattoos
loose holes in the ears

coquette she is, a mingling star. a voice so clear. a hairdo so impressive
she's an icon

praise yourself gaga mama, you've nothing to loose. you're old.

so she sang. sang so loud the song of darkness, yet her voice resonated light only.
sang across the plaza where water was filled into bottles, source for humans.
source attracting mankind.

you dive. you sparkle while you fly and especially so when you crash.
the water swallows you in the sinking weightless plunge of limbs and soul.
you look up. from there you see the sun. the child's world of vastness.
not boxes but beaches. you're under water. it's your platform from the ocean.
the sun is the parameter for the distance of the universe

you inhabitant
playing the spheres
have beauty and you hold power
with your senses you reflect

transgressional ghostly energy
can u trip on this? do you need pictures?

i like different cultures of indulgence.

                              waveye
                              whats not meditation?

the water hurts the eyes surely. close them
remember the view and cherish access.

captivating mental outlooks

trip it to the I-level and dance fun to our worlds rhythm

i have a couple of dates with the world.
she calls everyday with moments of mankind and nature

captivating love.

it's been spoiled it's been spoiled it's been spoiled
let go from this

it reappears
people run
they're weak. they're up for funtimes only lonely strong and thoughtful gun
you pierce their souls and manage holes to dig inside
and feature strength so trusting and so calm
afar the darkest doubt anchored in disbelief dissolves
blindingly progressive the world responds
light shines upon all
light

live detachment.
bury it inside you and never look back.
fleeing the land forming new islands

when we meet again i cry since i remember and i am not recognising you.
transformation-causing-detachments

we are adult strangers in a functional world
keeping it constructional with a regard speaking painlessness

so sterile when eyes meet
when do you grow to join the feeling with the person
stop deploying means for rescue
emotional relief by not admitting to it
cheapest of the cheap

who would have thought that we deserve that
the machine the angry the lost

the farewell of my hand while you decisively step forward
embed my soul into your memory

when we stroke essence
we meant it

your eyes were the sea i've promised to
the waves i rode and the flow that persisted.

stop to nurture to sustain to move together
to know to carry to obtain eachother
in this wholeness a world means only
a huge one
a holy
shining chance for times to come to run together
climbing with breath in time
holding ones side
holding ones mind

preciously

no shadow left. disappearance, total absence
we met in dreams rather involuntary
in the parkway you were still running

grief, nothing left but an empty spot
where the heart is placed
inscriptions of your face shall fade
your lifeline parts on your palm to the right
we are realising
whatever we've performed, however intense the act
everything folds up
in the blankness of my panic mind i see nowhere to go
only where i strand and am alone

the 11th hour is a collaboration between jonathan hallam and anastasia freygang
the imagery revolves around the emotion of grief, hope for resurrection and paths
towards it

atunement commences in the mind, translates into the physical - the methaphors
in this series evoke states of connection to the elements

our immediate surroundings in this city are shown here, these places are ours

rooftops in whitechaple above feelings and blue rooms in limehouse
at anatum's abode - years were spent being together on these platforms

moving times that lead to unfoldment, apprehension and focus on the now

each photograph is available for purchase as a poster at
www.jonathanhallam.net

we thank luisa martelo for her help with the layout and graphic design
her work is to be found here: www.luisamartelo.com

special thanks to abraham winterstein for the veil installation and costume
at bedfordhouse and lee fukke, saul ham, anna novikova, lucas liccini and
charlotte wendy law for their support and feedback

ISBN number 978-0-9929868-0-3
published by 11th hour publications
printed and bound by lecturis in eindhoven, holland